Jack and Larry

Jack Graney and Larry, the Cleveland Baseball Dog

Barbara Gregorich

Philbar Books
Chicago, IL

ISBN-13:978-1467958011
ISBN-10:1467958018

Design by Robin Koontz
Cover photo courtesy of Margot Mudd and Perry Mudd Smith

Library of Congress Cataloging-in-Publication Data
Gregorich, Barbara
Jack and Larry: Jack Graney and Larry, the Cleveland Baseball Dog

For

Margot Mudd
Perry Mudd Smith
Fred Schuld

who so generously shared
their knowledge and stories with me

Foreword

Jack Graney was born in St. Thomas, Ontario, Canada, and played baseball for the Cleveland American League team (now known as the Indians) from 1910-1922. As leadoff batter, Jack's life was full of firsts, particularly first hit and first run scored in a game or a season.

He was also the first, and only, major league player to own a dog that was the team's official mascot. That dog was Larry, a bull terrier.

All major leaguers dream of winning their league's pennant, and beyond that, the World Series. The story of Jack Graney and Larry is the story of a man, a dog, a team, and the pursuit of the pennant: a pursuit filled with both joy and sorrow.

1912

Left Out

John Gladstone Graney,
better known as Jack,
comes from Ontario, Canada,
    where friends call him Glad.

Jack is glad for many things:
        to have family and friends
                and to play major league baseball
                for Cleveland.

But Jack is not glad about
everything. Something is
            missing.

        Jack bats left,
                throws left,
                        plays left field . . .

        and feels left out —
                left behind
                in the pennant race
                always nabbed by
                some other team,
                        never by the
                                Cleveland Naps.

And now, something else
makes Jack unglad —
        makes him fear
        he will be more left out
                than ever.

The Buzz of Rumors

On the train bound
for spring training,
    rumors buzz
like baseball-sized horseflies —
buzz that Cleveland will trade
    Jack to the Detroit Tigers.

Jack hears the rumors
    and swallows hard.

He has covered
Cleveland's left field
two full seasons,
    chasing down hard-hit liners
        in hot sun and cold drizzle.

His friends play here.
His heart soars here.
    Jack longs for *this* team
    to win the pennant.

As the train chugs south,
Jack is left wondering
what it will take
for Cleveland to win
    the pennant. He is left
    wondering if he will be
        part of it all.

From 1901 to the present, Cleveland has been home to an American League baseball team. From 1903-1914, this team was nicknamed the Naps.

Spring Training

After a long winter
Jack and his teammates stretch,

    stretch to remember,

remember how to hit
    the fastball
    and curve,
how to slide,
and how to field
    one-hoppers,
    two-hoppers,
        good hoppers,
        bad hoppers.

Jack snares the line drives,
hoping no bad hoppers
    bounce his way —
    no trade to Detroit
        or anywhere else.

But life throws everyone
a bad hopper
        or two
            or three,
Jack knows that . . .

knows that the unforeseen
and unexpected
    could cross his path
        any day.

Something New

The unexpected jumps at Jack,
then zooms away. The four-footed
black and white bullet
races across the outfield,
scatters dust through the infield,
bumps into the backstop, and stands there
                    panting.

The exuberant dog is a young bull terrier
          that the team trainer
          won on a bet and brought to
                    camp.

Jack watches Larry
gnaw baseball leather,
hurl himself against sweaty
shoes and socks in ecstasy,
and snag his teeth on woolen
                    uniforms.

          Jack knows dogs.
          He knows that Larry
          is learning how to be part of the
                    pack.

The trainer gives the dog
to the team, and the players
make Larry their official
                    mascot.

Doc White, trainer for the Cleveland Naps, won the bull terrier from Prince Hunley, chief bellhop at the Hollenden Hotel in downtown Cleveland. The dog was named Prince, then Tige, then Larry.

Reliable

Jack understands how to be
part of the pack —
    do your own job
    and help
    everybody else
    do theirs.

He bats leadoff, where
his job is to make
something
happen:
    slap a single,
    slam a double,
    earn a walk,
    get hit by a pitch
        if that's what it takes
        to reach first base.

Jack does his job and does
it well. He can be counted on
to play his hardest for the team.

    He works harder than ever,
    hoping he won't be traded.

When the photographer arrives
Jack lines up with his teammates
    for the official team picture.

Three Wrongs

Team photos glow with promise,
each player anticipating
        September sunshine.

The Naps pose for
their official photo —
        thirty-eight people
                and one proud dog.

The papers call Larry
a bulldog,
but they are wrong.
        Larry is a bull terrier.

The rumors are wrong, too.
        Jack Graney is not
        traded to Detroit.

A heavy load lifts
from Jack's heart.
        He smiles and laughs
        and babbles happily
                to reporters.

"I have a hunch,"
        he tells them,
        "a hunch that the Naps
                will win the pennant."

Now, he means.

This year.

Wrong, Jack.
Wrong.

Bad hoppers
ahead.

During the 1850s James Hinks of England crossbred bulldogs, white English terriers, bull-and-terriers, and Dalmatians. Within a decade he produced the modern-day bull terrier. The first bull terriers were imported to the U.S. around 1900.

Knockdown Pitch

Still with the team he loves,
Jack Graney repels pitches
    with a sturdy bat
    and plucks fly balls out of the sky
        with a well-worn glove.

Things are looking good.

And then, life lobs Jack
    two warmup
    warnings
        and one
        knockdown pitch,
as if to say,
    Good things don't
        come easy.

    In Chicago an umpire
    steps on Jack's stomach
        as he slides into second.
            Jack is in pain.

    In Boston something
    Jack eats gives him
        food poisoning.
            Jack is in more pain.

    In Detroit a batter
    smashes a line drive
    to left field.

The ball plummets
earthward too soon,
like a one-winged goose
calling it quits.

Jack dives for the ball headfirst
and hits the ground hard.

Twice Jack struggles to stand,
but he can't.
His right arm dangles,
broken at the shoulder.

Teammates and trainer rush out
to help Jack into the clubhouse.
He grits his teeth, bearing the pain
without a sound as the trainer
sets his broken bones . . .

sets them incorrectly, so that
back in Cleveland the team doctor
cracks the shoulder apart
and lines up the bones
a second time.

Jack and the bench spend
the rest of the the season
together.

On the Bench

Larry spends time
on the bench, too.
Sometimes under it.

Larry leaps onto
the long wooden seat
and licks
Jack's fingers and face.

Jack's team is on the field,
but Jack isn't. He strokes
Larry, talking to him.

Jack sees that Larry
never gives up.

The dog is an
optimist — today
is good and tomorrow
will be great.

Jack makes himself and Larry
happy by teaching Larry tricks —
Roll Over,
Sit Up,
Jump.

Larry sniffs Jack and smells
Jack's determination,
smells how hard Jack works
for the good of the team.

At the other end of the bench,
somebody observes.

The Manager

That somebody is
Napoleon Lajoie,
    stellar second baseman
    and team manager.

Team namesake, too —
    when Lajoie first arrived
    in Cleveland, the fans
    nicknamed the whole
    team after him, which
        is how they became
        the Naps.

When the incomparable Lajoie
first arrived in Cleveland,
    he was expected to lead
    a losing team
    to the pennant.

But even star players pulsating
immense volumes of heat and energy
cannot always ignite
their teammates —
    cannot always lead a team
        to a first place finish.

After ten years of trying,
    Lajoie has learned this
    bitter lesson.

        Something is missing.

Lajoie knows what it is.

He looks at Jack and believes
that Jack knows, too.

He looks at Larry and *knows*
that Larry knows.

Lajoie makes a seemingly small
decision that ends up
monumental.

Larry belongs to the whole team,
true. But the whole team can't
take Larry home.

Lajoie looks at Jack.
He points at Larry.

"Take him," he tells Jack.
"The dog is yours."

Napoleon Lajoie [LAJ-a-way] played major league ball from 1896-1916. His lifetime .338 batting average is the 18th highest. Sportswriters consider him the greatest second baseman of the first half of the 1900s. After the Baseball Hall of Fame was dedicated in 1939, Lajoie was the sixth player inducted.

The Dog is Jack's

Jack is thrilled
to have Larry,
 but along with the rush
  comes the responsibility.

What does it mean,
he wonders,
 that the team manager
 gave Larry to him?

Was it merely convenient
for Lajoie to hand the dog
over to Jack? Or did the great
man have a plan?

 Jack ponders this
 as he plays with Larry . . .
  feeds Larry . . .
   walks Larry . . .
    talks to Larry.

Jack ponders this
as he watches Larry
play with his teammates,
 making each one
  smile.

 The beginning of a plan
 starts to grow in Jack's
 mind. A plan for next
  season.

Season's End

Standing on the open deck
of the boat, Jack admits to himself
that he was very wrong about the Naps.
    They did not win the pennant.

    In fact, they finished thirty games
        out of first.

The ferry steams across Lake Erie
from Cleveland to Port Stanley,
Ontario, and from there
    Jack and Larry ride
    the streetcar home,
    Larry's toenails *clickity-clicking*
    on the brick road that leads
        to Jack's house.

Family and friends welcome Jack
home, glad that he is safe.

On the outside Jack looks safe,
but Larry senses something gnawing
    Jack on the inside.
    He licks Jack's hands and face.

Jack shares his fear with Larry —
fear that his shoulder might not heal right,
fear that he might never again
    play in the big leagues.

    Larry listens, but does not
        agree.

1913

Team Dog

Jack and Larry leave Canada
for Cleveland, where Larry inhales
the scent of each player,
    twitching his tail and planting
    his paws on each
      of them.

Jack shows his teammates
each new trick Larry
    has learned —
    jumping as high as Jack's shoulder,
      sitting on Jack's shoulders,
      balancing on Jack's head.

On the wooden platform,
waiting for the southbound train,
      the Naps take turns
      playing with Larry.

Jack makes sure
each player knows that Larry
    is not just Jack's dog,
      he is the team's dog, too —
      the official mascot
    of the Cleveland Naps.

Jack reminds them that they
are all proud of Larry and of
      themselves, and he hints
      that maybe they should study
    how Larry behaves.

Boarding the train,
Jack flexes his arm
    and stretches his shoulder,
    heading for the aches
        of spring training

    and the hope
    that his arm has healed.

Healed

Yes!
At spring training
Jack is glad to discover
        that his arm has healed
                perfectly —
        he can field,
                he can throw,
                        he can hit,
all well enough
for the major leagues.

Over the winter the Cleveland
owners have made changes
to the team. They have hired
a new manager to replace
Napoleon Lajoie, who still
plays second base.

        The new manager,
        Joe Birmingham,
        puts Jack back in
        left field.

And then Birmy
puts Larry on a leash
        and takes him for a walk,

                and maybe talks to him
                about team spirit.

Pack Animals

Jack and Larry,
Larry and Jack,
    they are man and dog,
    dog and man,
        and they are very much
        alike.

    Jack is built compact:
        five feet nine inches
        and 180 pounds.

    Larry stands sturdy,
        twenty inches high
        at the shoulder,
            50 pounds of bone
            and muscle.

    Jack and Larry are friendly,
        eager to please,
        inquisitive,
        inventive,
            hardworking but
            fun-loving.

Jack and Larry
    are out to make
        changes.

Missing From the Group

Jack considers the difference
between the Naps and
    the teams they play against,
    and he sees what
      is missing.

Togetherness is missing —
    magic togetherness
    that overcomes
    what looks like
    sure defeat
      and turns it into
      sure victory.

Jack hopes that
he and Larry
can change that —
    can build a team
    that thinks not
    like twenty-five players,
      but like one unit.
      Like a pack.

Larry seems to understand.

At first he sits only with Jack,
but as the season goes on,
    Larry sits with other players.
    He barks happily
    when they succeed,
      wags his tail wildly
      and leaps up and down

when they step
into the dugout
    after scoring
    a run.

    Everybody on the team
    relates to Larry.

Somebody Special

Shoeless Joe Jackson
is not everybody,
    he is a somebody
    special.

    Shoeless and Jack
    came to the Naps
    at the same time,
        but although they
        both play the outfield,
    Jack in left and
    Shoeless in center,
        they do not possess
        the same talents.

Jack is a good ballplayer.
He is steady, smart,
hard-playing and reliable.
His feet are on the ground,
he belongs to the earth.

    Shoeless is such a spectacular
    hitter and fielder that
    he seems to soar above the earth —
    certainly above ordinary
    major leaguers.

Will Shoeless Joe Jackson
accomplish what
Napolen Lajoie
could not?
    Will he help lead
        the Naps to
        the pennant?

The owners think so.
The fans think so.
His teammates think so.

If Larry could talk,
what would he say
about Shoeless Joe Jackson?

Joe Jackson got the nickname of "Shoeless Joe" when he played a minor league game in his bare feet. He entered the major leagues in 1908 and was traded to Cleveland in 1910. In 1911 he led the American League with a batting average of .408; in 1912 he led the league with 226 hits. His lifetime batting average of .356 is the third highest in baseball history.

Toodlin' with Shoeless

Dogs can't talk,
    but they can still show
    how they feel.

During spring training one day,
Larry is happy to ride with Jack
    in Shoeless Joe's new car.

The men look spiffy
in checked driving caps,
    and Shoeless wears
    a raccoon coat.

Larry looks sharp
in a studded leather collar
    and his own dog-hair coat.

In the open car
Larry sniffs the breeze,
    reading its many
    messages.

The breeze might hint
what the future holds,
    but it never gives exact
    answers.

Jack, Larry, Shoeless,
and the whole team
    head north to their
    destinies.

Entertaining the Fans

At home in League Park,
the Nap players
entertain their fans
    with leapfrog — a new trick
        they have taught Larry.

The players line up front
to back and bend forward.
        Larry leaps onto the back
            of the last player
        and from there to the back
            of the next, and the next,
                and the next, until he has
        touched each of them —
            until he has leapdogged
                everyone.

And the fans love it
and clap and shout
        because they want
            this team to win
                the pennant.

From 1901 through 1946, the Cleveland team played in League Park, which seated 21,414 fans. In 1947 the team moved to Cleveland Municipal Stadium. In 1994 the team owerns built a new stadium, Jacobs Field, whose name was changed to Progressive Field.

Team Photo

This team, like all
    major league teams,
    has its photo taken.

Sitting near Jack but
    not in front of him,
        Larry poses for the official
        Cleveland Naps team photo.

His eyes glistening
with intelligence
    and eagerness,
Larry stares straight
into the camera
    as if to say,
"We are major leaguers,
    we have what
        it takes."

Larry is confident,
    Larry is loved —

but somebody wants
    to take Larry
        away
            from
                Jack.

Unprincely Behavior

Prince Hunley, the man who
put Larry up for loss
on a bet, and did in fact
lose, now wants the bull terrier
back.

      Jack says No.

Jack and everybody else
on the team knows the sequence
of events:
      Prince Hunley lost the bull terrier
         to Doc White on a bet;

      Doc White brought the dog
         to spring training for the team;

      Napoleon Lajoie, team manager,
         gave the dog to Jack Graney.

Jack won't give Larry back,
      Larry is his dog.

So Prince Hunley sues Jack,
asking the judge to award Larry
      back to him.

      The judge listens
         to both sides.

Larry is there in court, too.
      He listens. He licks

Jack's hand and stands
almost on top of
Jack's feet.

Raising his right hand,
Jack swears he has told
the truth. When Jack drops
his hand, Larry leaps

straight up,
as high as Jack's shoulder,
and when he lands,
Larry barks and tugs
at his leash
as if to say,
"The sun is shining,
the grass is green,
things are hopping,
what are we doing
indoors?"

The judge rules that Larry
belongs to Jack Graney.

Jack walks out of
the courtroom a happy
man, reassured that Larry
won't be taken
from him.

Larry walks out looking
for something to chase —
squirrels, maybe.

Meeting the President

Wherever Larry goes, he is interested
in chasing squirrels. In June the
Naps travel to Washington, D.C.

The country has a new President,
and each time a new President
is elected, American League teams
pay him a visit the first time
        they travel to Washington to play
            the Senators.

President Thomas Woodrow Wilson
sits in the White House,
and on June 18 the Naps visit.
        Larry runs free, off his leash —

            Zip!

        Larry chases a squirrel
        up an oak tree
        on the White House lawn,
            barking louder than a hot dog vendor,
            scraping the tree with his toenails,
            hankering to catch that rodent.

Manager Joe Birmingham
orders Jack to leash Larry
        and tie him up outside —

            maybe Birmy fears
            Larry might lift a leg
                against a piece of priceless
                antique furniture
                inside the White House.

But before Jack can clip a leash
on Larry, an aide announces
that the President wants to meet
the Cleveland team and their mascot.

The Naps file into the White House
respectfully, but Larry pushes his way
forward and stares at the President.

> "So this is Larry,
> the Mascot?"
> asks President Wilson.

"Yes, sir," says Jack Graney.

> "My daughters tell me
> he is a very smart dog,"
> says the President.
> > "I am sorry I could not
> > have been there yesterday
> > to see him perform."

The Cleveland Naps thank
the President and file out
of his office.

Back on the White House lawn,
Larry most likely sniffs and wonders,

Where is that squirrel?

Famous, Famous, Famous!

After the meeting
reporters rush out stories
    as if bulldogs were biting
        the seats of their pants.

They inform the world
that Larry is the first dog
ever formally introduced
    to a President
        of the United States,

and from then on Larry is
famous, famous, famous!
And whenever reporters
write his name, *Larry,*
    they also write, *official mascot*
    of the Cleveland Naps, and
    they write, *the first dog to*
        meet the President of the U.S.A.

The words and the fame
do not swell Larry's head.

Larry does not read
    newspapers.

Team Player

You don't have to know how to read
in order to do the right thing.
    Larry knows the right thing
    and teaches it by
        example.

Just two days after
meeting the President,
    the bull terrier makes a
    bold move.

Manager Joe Birmingham
coaches third base,
where he apparently says something
to really annoy the umpire,
    who ejects Birmy
    from the
        game.

As Birmy returns
to the dugout,
    Larry rushes
    up the stairs
    and into the third-base
        box.

It appears that Larry intends
    to coach third
        base.

The umpire does not
agree and ejects Larry,
　　too, ordering him back to the
　　　　dugout.

Still, Larry has made his
point —

when one of the team
can't do the job,
　　another must
　　　　step in and take his
　　　　　　place.

Jack nods and thumps
　　Larry on the back in
　　　　approval.

Accidents

By the end of August,
it looks as if, maybe,
  the Naps have learned
  what it takes to be
  a team.

They enter September
  with a chance to take
  the lead.

But on the train bound
for Washington,
  Cy Falkenberg and
  Vean Gregg, the Naps'
  two best pitchers, get into
    a wrestling match with
      each other
    and injure
      each other
    and are unable
      to pitch.

When a team member
injures himself, he hurts
  the whole team even more.

The Naps end up losing
games they should have won.
  They finish the season third —
  nine games out of
    first place.

Jack and his best friends on the
team, catcher Steve O'Neill
and shortstop Ray Chapman,
are deeply disappointed.

Jack knows that
life supplies
many accidents,
some happy,
some horrible.

No need to create
your own accidents —
no need to derail
yourself.

1914

Riding the Rails

While the Naps play cards
and tell tales to reporters
on their southbound train,
    Larry travels in his own box
    in the baggage car —
    the railroads do not allow
        animals to travel
            in passenger cars.

    There is safety
    with the group,
        danger in being
           alone.

A railroad worker couples
Larry's baggage car
to the wrong train.

    The Cleveland Naps
    chug to one destination
        while their mascot
        chugs to another.

When the Naps arrive
at spring training,
    Larry is
        missing.

To the Rescue

Jack runs to the railroad depot.
"Find Larry," he demands.
"Give him water
        to drink.
Give him food
        to eat."

Jack telegrams,
Jack phones,
Jack makes the railroad understand
        that Larry
                is in danger.

A railroad worker finds Larry's
baggage car and Larry's box.
He lets Larry out,
        gives him water
                and food.

Then Larry is put back
into his box and this time
he is shipped
        in the right
                direction.

Two days later
Larry's long ride
ends. He races toward
        his teammates and leaps
                into Jack's arms.

Protecting Jackets

Back with his pack,
Larry enjoys his days.
He prances, he springs, he races
around corners like a major leaguer.

He leaps high into the air
as if snagging a long
line drive. Larry is always
pumped, looking for something
to do, something or someone to
investigate.

Fans wander around
the spring training camp,
checking out the players,
asking for autographs.

Some fans are honest
and some are not.

Southern sun warms
the players and they toss
their baseball jackets aside.
That's when some so-called
fan, someone who claims
to love the players,
tries to steal a jacket.

Out of nowhere
Larry charges,
his deep bark and
thick body scaring
the would-be thief halfway
to Cleveland, causing him
to flee without
the baseball jacket
which wasn't his
anyway.

Larry's dangerous ride
in the boxcar did not
leave him confused —
he knows his team
and how to
protect it.

Jumpers

Not everybody knows their team
and how to work for it.

During the off-season,
the Naps best pitcher,
Cy Falkenberg, who won
twenty-three games
the previous year, and who
would have won more
if he hadn't been horsing around,
        abandons the Naps — jumps
    to the new Federal League
            for bigger money.

Falkenberg did not identify
with the team, only with
the salary.

The Naps enter the season
without a strong
        pitching staff.

The Federal League was a third major league that began with
the 1914 season and ended after the 1915 season. The owners
of Federal League teams lured ballplayers from the National and
American Leagues by paying higher salaries. Weeghman Field was
built in Chicago for the Federal League Chicago Whales. After the
Federal League folded, the Chicago Cubs played in Weeghman,
which was renamed Wrigley Field.

Goat

The Naps start the season
with a fan who drags
a goat to League Park
on Opening Day
         and presents the animal
                  to Manager Joe Birmingham.

Does this fan
think a goat can
         frolic with the players,
         sit on their laps,
         ride in their automobiles,
         chase away thieves,
         play leapfrog,
                  and meet the President
                  of the United States?

Larry chases the goat
off the field.

But the Naps lose the game.

By the end of May
the team is ten games out.

By the end of June . . .
fifteen.

New Pitcher

The team is not
playing well, but Jack
        does not slack off.
He knows you can never
convince others to do their best
        unless you always do your best.

In Boston's Fenway Park,
Jack is the first to face
a young Red Sox pitcher —
        George Herman Ruth,
                better known as Babe.

With the count three-and-two,
        Jack drives a hit
                through the infield.

Jack Graney enters
baseball records with two firsts —
        first batter to face Babe Ruth
        and first player to collect a hit
                off the soon-to-be famous Bambino.

But the Naps
lose the game —
        another road trip loss
        in a string of many.

Babe Ruth, who started out as a pitcher, played major league
baseball from 1914-1935. As an outfielder, he dominated baseball
during the 1920s. Ruth was the first player to hit 60 home runs in
one season. His lifetime batting average of .342 is tenth highest in
baseball history. The Red Sox traded Ruth to the Yankees in 1919.

Taking Care of Business

When the team is on the road
Larry sleeps in the same hotel room
  as Jack and Jack's on-the-road
  roommate, shortstop Ray Chapman.

Jack and Ray have a bathroom,
  but Larry does not.

No problem.

Larry scratches at the door
  and Jack or Ray let him out.

Larry barks at the elevator
and somewhere down below
  the elevator operator hears
  and responds.

The elevator arrives,
the door opens,
  and Larry steps in.

    The door closes
    and down they go.

On the lobby level
Larry sniffs out the bellman,
  who opens the back door.

In every major league city,
the hotel workers know
  and love Larry.

Larry steps outside
to do his business.

He probably explores
the alleys and back
streets, because Larry
        is a dog and dogs
        are curious about
                scents and sights.

When he's ready, Larry
returns to the hotel.
        Bellman lets him in,
        operator takes him up,
                Jack and Ray welcome
                him back.

Larry is an intelligent,
confident dog.

He sits and listens
to Jack and Ray
        talk about the team.

Despite Jack's hopes
and plans, the magic
        togetherness

is still missing —
        really, *really* missing.

The Basement

Woe, woe, woe,
the Cleveland Naps finish
    the season in last
        place,

way, way, *way*
down in the
    basement—

forty-eight-and-a-half games
behind the winners.

The team's one-hundred-and-two losses
    and fifty-one wins
        are an all-time worst record
            for the Cleveland
                American League team.

Larry feels the team's
    dejection
        and buries his head
            between his
                paws.

Not Even a Name

And then, at the end
of the horrible season,
at the end
of the black-hole finish,
the owners trade
Napoleon Lajoie
to the Philadelphia Athletics.

With Napoleon gone,
the team doesn't even
have a name.

The average playing span
of a major leaguer is ten years.
Jack has been a major leaguer
five years already. He wonders
whether Cleveland will win
the pennant during his playing
years — or ever.

On the way home
to Canada,
Larry licks Jack's hand
and tugs at his pant legs.

Never give up,
he seems to say.

Never give up.

1915

San Antonio Bulldog

The Cleveland owners
choose San Antonio, Texas,
as the site of spring training,
  maybe thinking that a new site
  will bring new might
  to their last-place group.

After practice Jack goes
golfing with teammate
Terry Turner, and of course
Larry accompanies them.

Another golfer also brings a dog —
  a ferocious bulldog that attacks
  Larry!

Larry fights back.
The dogs whirl around
  like a load of black and white
  laundry, teeth clicking,
  claws clacking.

The bulldog is heavy-duty,
with dragon-sharp teeth
  and a mouth wide enough
  to swallow a bat sideways.

The bulldog hurts Larry bad,
but Larry will not quit.

His teammates rush in
to help — Jack punches
        the attacker with his fists,
        and Terry breaks a golf club
        over the bulldog's thick head.

Jack and Terry rush Larry
to a vet, who stitches
        a wide piece of chomped-off hide
        back to Larry's side.

The vet also sews up
a deep bite in Larry's neck.

        Larry licks his wounds,
        one sorry-looking dog.

If Larry's experience
is any sign of what
is to come, the team
        is not yet able
        to defeat
        outsiders.

A New Name

Part of shaping a team
is giving it a name.
      Self-identity and pride
      come from a name.
Larry is Larry,
and Jack is Jack —

but who is the Cleveland team
      now that Napoleon Lajoie
      is gone?

The Cleveland sports writers
name the team
      the Cleveland Indians.

What an opportunity
they missed —

they could have avoided
insulting American Indians:
      they could have named
      the team the Cleveland
      Bull Terriers.

Sorry

Larry recovers from his wounds
and ceases to be sorry-looking.
    Not so the Cleveland team,
    which is especially sorry —

sorry to lose its thirty-second
game of the season by June 20,

        sorry that few fans
        show up to lessen the
        pain.

By July 15 Cleveland has lost
forty-nine unhappy games.

        Spirits sink low.

        Tempers glow red.

And not just human
        tempers.

Frenzy

It is true that bull terriers are strong,
it is true they are quick,
it is true they are loyal—
> it is also true that sometimes
> the snippy terrier side
> of the family tree
> takes over.

All day long Larry fetches balls,
guards caps, jackets, and gloves,
chases intruders off the field,
> all of this in the hot, hot sun
> with fans booing,
> the team losing,
> and the smell of unavailable
> hot dogs everywhere.

Larry foams himself into a frenzy,
racing everywhere to do everything
at once in true terrier style.

> He growls.
> He snarls at one
>> teammate
>> and snaps at
>> another.

Larry needs
> a rest.

By Sea and By Land

Jack knows what Larry needs —
    time to rest and play,
    time to be just a dog,
        not an official mascot.

Jack walks Larry
to the Cleveland dock
    and puts him on the ferry
    bound for Port Stanley.
        Jack waves goodbye
    and Larry barks
    See you soon to Jack.

Sitting in the wheelhouse
with the captain, Larry
    thumps his tail eagerly.
        Ferry whistle blowing,
        the boat steams off.

On the other side
of Lake Erie, the boat docks
    and Larry trots down the ramp
    to where the trolly conductor
    waits for him. Everybody in Port Stanley
        knows Larry the bull terrier.

Larry scampers aboard the trolley
and stares out the window
at the orchards,
    sniffing the apple smells.
    He barks at the deer,
    and of course he jumps off
        at the right stop.

Larry's toenails make happy noises
as he trots down the brick street.
　　He walks up to the correct house,
　　barks by the door,
　　and is welcomed home by
　　　　Jack's parents.

　　Love,
　　　　Trust,
　　　　　　Loyalty —

beautiful to give,
beautiful to receive.

Say It Ain't So!

When Larry returns to Cleveland,
he immediately sniffs
that somebody is missing.
        The Cleveland owners have
        sold their greatest player,
                Shoeless Joe Jackson.

This is fine with Shoeless,
who does not feel loyal to Cleveland,
who wants to win a World Series ring
        but no longer believes
        his Cleveland teammates
                can do it.
Off he goes to what he thinks
is a better future with
the Chicago White Sox.

After Shoeless is traded,
Cleveland fans do not bother
        coming to the ballpark to boo.
        They stay away altogether.

But a team needs the roar
of the crowd, needs somebody —
        tens of thousands of somebodies —
                to believe in it.

Cleveland finishes
a sorry seventh,
        only one step up
                from the
                        bottom.

1916

Nothing to It

Standing in a circle,
flexing chest and shoulder muscles,
the players grunt as they heave
a heavy medicine ball
back and forth —
      Terry to Jack
           to Steve, to Ray
              to Terry.

Larry watches, tail thumping.

Somebody drops the ball and
      Larry swoops in.

Teeth gripping the sphere,
strong jaw clamped shut,
Larry prances down the field,
tossing his head as if to say —

      What's with all the grunting
           and groaning?

In any pack, there is always
somebody who does a certain
something better than
      the other members.

That, in fact, is good
      for the team.

A New Leftie

After two very low seasons,
the Cleveland team wishes
    it had a lot of somebodies
        who did things best.

And then Tris Speaker
of the Boston Red Sox
    is traded to Cleveland.

Like Jack, Tris bats left,
    throws left, and plays
        the outfield.

The new center fielder
can do it all —
    slap singles,
    wallop doubles,
    smash triples.

Tris's fingers glitter with
not one
    but two
    World Series rings,
    both of which he won
    with the Red Sox.

Tris craves a third ring.

The rest of the team craves
    a first.

Is Tris the answer?
Will Speaker spark
    the fire that burns
      a path
        to the pennant?

Jack hopes so.

And then Jack keeps
on doing the things he
    has been doing
      to help build
        the team.

Nicknamed "The Gray Eagle," Tris Speaker helped the Red Sox win the 1912 and 1915 World Series. He was traded to Cleveland in 1916 when he refused to take a pay cut with Boston. Speaker ended his 22-year major league career with a .345 batting average, the sixth highest in baseball history. He holds the lifetime record for most doubles: 792.

Dog Gone

Everything that Jack wants,
Larry wants, too. Dogs are so smart
that they know what humans want.
> They study humans' tiniest
> movements, watch where their eyes
> look and decide for themselves
> what that means.

When Cleveland plays the Washington
Senators, Cleveland wants the Senator
batters to strike out. Maybe Larry
senses this, or maybe the players train
him, but whatever the reason,
> when a Senator batter is in a tight
> spot, say a count of three balls
> and two strikes, Larry waits
> until the Cleveland pitcher hurls
> the baseball,
>> and then Larry
>> *howls* —

howls long and loud.

The howling disturbs
the batter and maybe makes
him miss as he swings.

The Cleveland players
and Larry enjoy
> this little game.

But the Senators do not,
and they complain
to the American league umpires
        and the American League President —
        who bans Larry
                from Griffith Stadium!

Larry becomes not only the first
dog to meet the President, but also
        the first dog banned from
        a baseball stadium.

Even though Larry isn't with them,
the players know what to do.
        When a Senator batter has a full count,
        they wait until the pitch is on its way,
        then they shout, "Swing!" or "Can't hit!"

In their own way, they howl
        to help build the team.

First Number One

Some firsts are important
and some are just fun,
        but both help build morale.

In baseball's early days
players wear uniforms,
        they wear attitudes,
        and they wear down . . .

but they do not wear
names or numbers.

On June 26, though,
in a game against Chicago,
        the Cleveland players
        pin numbers
        to their sleeves.

As leadoff batter,
Jack wears number one,
        becoming the first
        major leaguer
        to bat while wearing
        a number on his
                uniform.

In 1916 no other team seemed interested in numbers on uniforms,
so Cleveland dropped the idea. In 1929 the New York Yankees
stitched numbers on the back of each player's uniform: thus the
Yankees are credited with introducing uniform numbers to baseball.

The Circle

Another morale booster
is showing the home fans
Larry's many tricks.

Larry fetches,
        leapdogs,
                sits up and begs,
and when a Cleveland player commands,
"Play dead, Larry,"
the bull terrier
                keels
                        over.

On some days
Jack and Larry
perform the special trick
        that shows how perfectly
        they understand
                each other.

Jack leans over, creating
a circle with his arms.

Larry looks and leaps
        through the heart of that
                loving circle.

Tris, Jack, and the Future

Jack has a good feeling as
Larry leaps through the circle,
        a feeling that Cleveland is
                on its way.

Jack's good feeling increases
the power of his bat: he racks up
record numbers. For each double Tris
smashes, Jack smashes one, too,
        and when the season is over,
        Jack and Tris have each slammed
                forty-one doubles —
        the American League best
                for the year.

For the first time,
Jack has led the league
        in a batting category.

Not only that, but Jack
scores one-hundred-and-six runs
in the season,
        second only to Ty Cobb's
        one-hundred-and-thirteen runs.

The Cleveland team
wins seventy-seven games
        and loses seventy-seven games,
                finishing fifth.

But this is not
a hopeless fifth,
    it is fourteen games
    out of first place,
and Jack believes
and Tris believes
    that the team can whittle
    fourteen down to nothing
    next season.

They anticipate good things
for Cleveland.

    They do not anticipate
    sorrow.

1917

Another First

Second base is icing,
but first is the cake,
and without the cake
there is no meaningful meal.

Leadoff batters face one main
task —
reach
first
base.

In the first game of the season,
Jack Graney delivers —
he reaches first base.

A teammate drives him home
and Jack scores
Cleveland's first run
of the season.

Looks Like a Team

Cleveland is looking good.
Very, very good.

Wambsganss covers second,
Chapman safeguards short,
Graney patrols left,
     Speaker swoops across center,
     and O'Neill shields home plate.
Bagby, Coveleski, and Morton
     pitch, and pitch,
          and pitch.

The Cleveland players
suddenly realize their power—
     they are a nine-cylinder engine
     eager to roar down the road,
     blow away traffic,
          and cross the finish line
               first.

Winning comes easy
sometimes, but mostly
     the path is filled with
          pain.

A big sadness
will fall like soot
     all over Jack Graney,
          all over the team.

Looks Like a Loss

On May 26 five thousand home fans
watch Cleveland play the New York
Yankees.

> Bottom of the ninth,
> Cleveland behind five
> > zip.

Four thousand fans
> walk away.

Larry does not like this.

> He paces the dugout,
> his toenails *click, click, clicking.*
> > He studies his pack
> > and barks encouragement —

> *Do not quit!*

> *Do not roll over*
> > *and play dead!*

Triple Steal and Bite

The game is not over.

In the bottom of the ninth
Cleveland loads the bases.
The Yankee pitcher throws,
and before you can say
           "Yankees win,"
           all three Cleveland runners
           steal a base —
                   from first to second,
                        second to third,
                             third to home!

A triple steal!

This rattles the Yankees,
who go to pieces
           as the remaining fans go wild
           and the Cleveland players
                just go on scoring.

The magic is there —
magic togetherness that overcomes
           what looks like sure defeat
           and turns it into
                sure victory.

Cleveland wins the game!

Jubilation!

Celebration!

Larry jumps up and down,
barks and pants,
    and bites the pants
    of the team Vice President,
    nearly ripping them off
        in his
            excitement.

Bad Hop Ahead

Cleveland plays one
good hop game
after another,

       racing down the road
          to victory.

A bad hop
lurks ahead,
but nobody
knows it.

       Bad hops do not send
       telegrams saying
       they are
          on the way.

Lost

Jack and Larry saunter into
downtown Cleveland's
Rose Building.

Jack steps off the elevator,
but when he looks around
        Larry is not there.
        The elevator is gone
                and so is Larry.

Jack looks for his dog
for a long, long time.

He cannot find him
        anywhere.

Jack doesn't want to leave,
but he must. The team
        must board the train
        to Washington, D.C.

Jack begs family and friends
and everybody he can think of
        to look for Larry.

            "Find him," says Jack.
            "And call me."

Stray Dog

Larry wanders out there
in the streets and alleys,
    down by the river
    where old buildings creak
        and mean dogs snarl.

A stray dog attacks him.

Larry does not run,
    he is not a quitter,
        he fights back.

When Larry is finally found,
    the damage is
        too deep.

Friends rush Larry
to the vet's office,

    but the vet
    cannot cure him.

A Hard Rain

In Washington a hard, dark rain
pounds the city and floods
the ballpark. No game today,
make it up tomorrow.

> Jack and his teammates
> slouch in the hotel lobby,
>   staring at the gloom.

Telegram for Jack Graney.

Jack rips it open and learns
        that Larry has died.

> Heavy rain batters
>   Jack's heart.

Teammates lay their arms
around Jack, around each other.

> Their friend is gone.

Cleveland loses five games
to Washington.

> Jack and the team
>   stumble in deep
>   sorrow.

Goodbye, Larry

Life has thrown Jack
a bad hopper.

Jack understands that time
will help smooth
the sharp hurts
that jut through his heart.

But he knows, too,
that there will never
be another dog like
Larry.

Never.

The most famous animal mascot in the world is dead. It's Larry, Jack Graney's [bull terrier].

Larry toured the big league circuit with Graney and the rest of the Cleveland team scores of times. . . . He performed amusing stunts for thousands of fans in every park in the circuit.

Porters on trains and in hotels afforded him courtesies that would do honor to any doggy heart.

In between his trips with the team Larry crossed the international boundary into Canada a score of times, Graney sending him home to St. Thomas, Ont., for vacations occasionally.
— Cleveland Press, July 26, 1917

Still Standing

Sometimes it seems
that life is a tornado
    that swoops us up,
    slaps us around,
and drops us,
black and blue
    but still standing.

At season's end
the Cleveland team
    is still standing.

They finish third.

As each man returns
home, he wonders . . .

will his team ever
    ever,
        ever
            capture

    the American League
        pennant?

1918-1919

So Close

All of Jack and Larry's
hard work helped
build a team.

In 1918 Ray Chapman
scores the most runs
of the American League
season, and Tris Speaker
wallops the most doubles.

In 1918 Cleveland comes so
close to the pennant,
finishing two-and-a-half
games behind Boston.

The Red Sox go on
to win the World Series
        against the Chicago Cubs.

First But Still Second

In 1919 Jack Graney leads
the American League in
bases-on-balls, earning
        one-hundred-and-five
        walks for his team.

Jack is always there,
doing his job,
        getting on base,
        letting his teammates
        bring him home
                to win games.

For ten years Jack has seen
the pennant as a flag
        that Cleveland can win.

He has learned that we do not travel
through life in straight lines,
        we travel in zigs and zags, forward
        and backward and sometimes
                we stand still.

Cleveland finishes
second again, just behind
the Chicago White Sox,
        who are expected to
        pulverize Cincinnati
                in the World Series.

In the Back

The whole baseball world,
including of course Jack
and his teammates, is

        stunned.

It looks to everybody
as if certain White Sox
players are deliberately

        losing,

deliberately losing games
and stabbing their own
teammates in the

        back.

After the Cincinnati Reds
win the World Series,
the outrage begins and

        swells.

Eight White Sox players
are brought to trial
for working with gamblers
to "fix" the outcome of the

        games.

One of these players is
Shoeless Joe Jackson.
He and the other seven
are banned from baseball

        forever.

Jack Graney and his teammates
can't understand how a ballplayer
could do such a thing
    to his
        teammates
    to his
        fans
    to
        himself.

Jack and his teammates
crave a pennant, yearn to play
in a World Series — and if
they get the chance,
they will not
    spit
        on it.

1920

Start Here

Two seasons in second place
      mean nothing to the season
        of spring.

Spring is a forward-pointing
arrow that commands:
      Start Here.

Jack and his teammates
leap into the game
      much like Larry
        used to leap
        across their backs.

They win.

They win again and again,
facing tough competition
      from the Yankees
        and the White Sox.

Jack and his team
don't know it yet,
      but they will face
      tougher than that.

      They will lose
        part of themselves
          once again.

A Crushing Blow

Cleveland wins first place
and keeps it, roaring
toward the end of the line
        like a well-stoked
        freight train.
                And then . . .

On August 16 Cleveland
faces the Yankees
        in Yankee Land.

Submarine pitcher Carl Mays
fires an inside pitch
to Ray Chapman,
        who is crowding the plate.

The pitch hits Chappy
in the head.
He collapses.
        His teammates rush forward
        and carry him off the field.

Twelve hours later Ray Chapman dies,
        killed by a pitch.

        The team's shortstop,
        Jack's best friend,
                is gone.

Ray Chapman, 1891-1920, joined the Cleveland team in 1912. In 1917 he stole 52 bases: a Cleveland record until 1980. In 1918 he led the American League in walks and in runs scored. Thousands of Clevelanders attended Chapman's funeral.

A Strong Grip

The team staggers —
        too shocked,
        too sad,
        too confused
        to win.

They lose first place,
        they slip,
                they slide,
                        they fall further
                                and further behind.

Manager Tris Speaker
knows he must lead the way.
        He hits and fields hard,
                as if he doesn't hurt.

Jack knows that life
hands out cruel loss.
        But Jack won't let loss
        reduce him to sawdust,
        to be scattered on the basepaths
                of history
                        and blown away.

Jack urges his teammates
        forward.
Their magic togetherness
        returns.

Cleveland chomps down
     and gets a grip
     on the pennant —
     a grip as strong as that
        of a bull terrier.

By mid-September
     the team has fought
     its way back
        to first place.

The Winners Circle
is in sight
     and the team
     does not quit
        until it stands
           inside.

At last,
     at last,
        at *last*!

Cleveland wins
     the pennant!

Game One

The World Series is
a best-of-nine this year,
      meaning it takes five
      victories to win those
      championship rings.

Cleveland's opponents
are the Brooklyn Robins,
      who do not have as good
      a record, but who are
      tough fighters.

The first three games are played
      in Brooklyn.

With Stan Coveleski
on the mound,
      Cleveland comes away
      with a 3-1 victory.

Games Two and Three

In Ebbets Field, across the river
from where Ray Chapman died,
    the Cleveland team is uneasy,
      its heart heavy.

Brooklyn wins
    games two and three.

Jack and his teammates
ride the rails
    back to their home
    town for the next
      four games.

Larry does not ride
in the boxcar as he used to,
Chappy does not joke and play cards
as he used to . . .

    but Chappy and Larry live
      in the hearts of their team.

Game Four

Homecrowd roars wake
all of Ohio
  as Stan Coveleski
  pitches another full game,
  leading Cleveland
    to a 5-1 victory.

The Series is tied,
two games all,

and if people could see
into the future, all
  of Cleveland would close down
    to watch
    Game Five.

Game Five

Jack Graney has seen a lot
of firsts in his baseball life,
but none as exciting as
the firsts of Game Five.

The first first is this:

> In the first inning
> Cleveland right fielder Elmer Smith
> clobbers a grand slam — the first
> grand slam in World Series history.

The second first is this:

> In the fourth inning
> Cleveland pitcher Jim Bagby slugs
> a home run — the first homer
> by a pitcher in World Series history.

The third first is this:

> In the fifth inning
> Cleveland second baseman
> Bill Wambsganss turns
> an unassisted triple play —
> the first and only one
> in World Series history!

The crowd goes wild.

Larry would have gone wild, too,
would have barked and jumped
and jumped and barked
and torn the pants off of
everybody.

Cleveland wins 8-1
and leads the Series
three games to two

Unassisted triple plays are among the rarest feats in baseball.
Wamby's unassisted triple play went like this: (1) he caught a line
drive; (2) he stepped on second to force out the runner who had
been there; (3) he tagged out the runner arriving from first base.

Game Six

Cleveland sends a late-season
addition to the mound,
        Duster Mails.

Even though Duster
hasn't been with the team
        the whole season,
        the magic has kissed
                him, too.

Cleveland wins
the game 1-0.

Game Seven

Jack Graney sits on the bench
and smiles about
his past predictions.
  He laughs with joy,
  knowing what will
   happen.

Victory will taste sweet
but not syrupy,
  toughened by tears
  for those no longer here.

Jack and his teammates
feel their own strength
  as they take the field.

For the third time
in this World Series,
  Stan Coveleski takes
  the mound. He pitches
  a complete game,
   leading Cleveland
   to a 3-0 shutout.

Cleveland sweeps
all four home games —

  Cleveland wins
  the World Series!

1921-78

Goodbye, Uniform

Jack is satisfied.
He did his best
to help build a team
     that captured the pennant
     and won
     the World Series.

When the 1922 season ends,
he retires.

But Jack is not done
with the game he loves.

Another first
waits . . .

     down the road . . .

          in the distance.

First Again

In 1932 Jack is first again —
he becomes radio broadcaster
        for Cleveland games,
        the first former major leaguer
                to turn sports announcer.

Fans listen to Jack because
he can describe the stadiums
and playing fields for them —
        Jack played in those stadiums
                and on those fields.

In 1948 Cleveland wins
another pennant and another
        World Series, and Jack is glad
        to be there, describing it all.

When Jack retires in 1953,
players and fans
        celebrate Jack Graney Night,
        to honor the man who
                did so much to build
                their team.

The young fans remember
Jack's voice broadcasting
        the game from the time
        they were toddlers.

The old fans remember
Jack as a player
    and as the man who loved
        Larry.

All that Jack contributed
    is valued in hearts
        as big as his own.

In 1984 Jack Graney was inducted into the Canadian Baseball Hall of Fame. In his honor the CBHOF created a broadcasting award called the Jack Graney Award. It is presented to a member of the news media who has made a great contribution to the game of baseball through his life's work.

As did Jack.

Jack and Larry

In his house Jack Graney
hung pictures on the wall —
       pictures of himself
              and Larry.

For no matter
how many years
Larry had been gone,
       he always lived
              in Jack's heart —

playing leapdog,
       fetching baseballs,
              and jumping
              through

                     that loving circle

              of Jack's arms.

Barbara Gregorich studied at Kent State University, the University of Wisconsin, and Harvard. Before becoming a writer she worked as an English instructor, a typesetter and a letter carrier. Her children's books include many Start-to-Read titles such as *Jog, Frog, Jog* and *The Gum on the Drum* for School Zone Publishing; Workman's *Brain Quest Workbook: Grade 4*; ghostwriting for the Boxcar Children series; and the early readers *Waltur Buys a Pig in a Poke and Other Stories*, and *Waltur Paints Himself into a Corner and Other Stories*, both from Houghton.

Her titles for adults include *She's on First*, a baseball novel; and *Dirty Proof* and *Sound Proof*, mystery novels. Her adult nonfiction, *Women at Play: The Story of Women in Baseball*, won the SABR-Macmillan Award for Best Baseball Research of the Year in 1993. Even though *Women at Play* is an adult title, kids ages ten and older have read the book. Barbara wrote *Jack and Larry* for kids, but many adults will find that this heartfelt true story from baseball history is for them, too.

Barbara lives in Chicago with her husband, Phil Passen, who plays the hammered dulcimer. Her web site is www.barbaragregorich.com

Made in the USA
Lexington, KY
12 February 2012